THE VALUE OF HUMOR

The Story of Will Rogers

VALUE COMMUNICATIONS, INC.
PUBLISHERS
LA JOLLA, CALIFORNIA

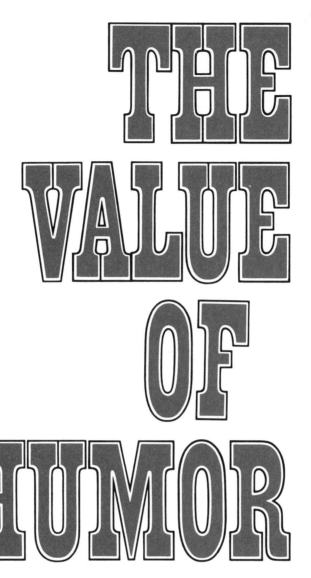

THE VALUE OF HUMOR

The Story of
Will Rogers

BY SPENCER JOHNSON, M.D.

ILLUSTRATED BY STEVE Pileggi

THE DANBURY PRESS

The Value of Humor is part of the ValueTales series.

The ValueTale of Will Rogers Text copyright © 1976 by Spencer Johnson, M.D. Illustrations copyright © 1976 by Value Communications, Inc.

First Edition
Manufactured in the United States of America
For information write to: Value Tales, P.O. Box 1012
La Jolla, CA 92038

Library of Congress Cataloging in Publication Data

Johnson, Spencer.
    The value of humor.

    SUMMARY: One in a series of works which demonstrate the importance of various values. In this work a biography of Will Rogers illustrates the value of humor.
    1.   Rogers, Will, 1879-1935—Juvenile literature.
2.   Entertainers—United States—Biography—Juvenile literature.   3.   Humorists, American—Biography—Juvenile literature.   [1.   Rogers, Will, 1879-1935.   2.   Entertainers.   3.   Humorists.   4.   Wit and humor]   I.   Title.
PN2287.R74J6   791'.092'4 [B] [92]   76-41782
ISBN 0-916392-05-8

Dedicated to
Uncle Bud who taught his
young nephew the value of humor
and Charlie and Cindy
who made this book possible

This tale is about a very humorous person, Will
Rogers. The story that follows is based on events
in his life. More historical facts about Will Rogers
can be found on page 63.

Once upon a time...

there lived a man named Will Rogers. He was loved and admired by almost everybody. People even built a statue of him.

They loved Will so much because he had learned to do something special. He learned to do it very well. He even showed lots of other people how to do it. What do you think it was?

Well, it all began when he was a little boy.

NEVER MET A MAN I DIDN'T LIKE

Young Will lived on his parents' ranch in Oklahoma. Like most children, he liked to play and have fun instead of doing his chores. Sometimes he would let his pony swim in the cool stream. He would hang onto the pony's tail and laugh.

One day Will thought, "There's something I'd like to do that would be even more fun."

"Would you teach me how to rope?" Will asked Dan Walker. Dan was a cowboy who worked on the ranch, and he could lasso just about anything that moved with his lariat. "I'd like to be the best roper in the world," said Will.

"Oh dear!" thought Will's mother when she heard this. "Whatever will become of Will? I'd like to see him grow up and become a minister and help people, but all he wants to do is twirl a rope."

Will began to spend a lot of time playing with his lariat. By now, his father wasn't too pleased with him either. One day his father called, "Will, come here!"

"Oh, oh!" thought Will.

"You're playing when you should be doing your chores, young man," scolded Will's father. "You're a good boy, Will, but you must work. In fact," said his father kindly, "you must work very hard if you want to do something well."

Will felt sad because he had displeased his father. He went off by himself.

Will sat quietly on a fence and tossed his lariat. He thought about what his father had said. "I wish I never got into trouble with my mom and dad," he thought. "I wish I always did the right thing."

As Will swung his lariat, he heard the humming sound that a twirling rope always makes as it spins through the air. But Will pretended that the hum was really the rope talking to him.

And then it happened!

"Howdy, Will," the rope seemed to say. "I'm Larry—Larry Ett. I'd like to be your best friend."

"Wow!" exclaimed Will. He jumped down off the fence and shouted, "I'd love to have a best friend like you!"

Of course everyone knows that your best friend is yourself. Will knew that he had made up Larry Ett, and that he was really just talking to himself. But it was more fun to think of his rope as his friend.

Larry Ett grinned. "Okay," he said. "We're partners. Now listen, partner, and I'll tell you something that might make you feel better."

"What's that?" asked Will.

13

"You need a good laugh," said Larry Ett.
"That'll perk you up in no time."

"I don't feel like laughing," Will protested.
He went into the house and sat on his bed.

"The times you don't feel like laughing are
the times you need to laugh the most,"
said Larry Ett. "Anybody can laugh when
he's having fun. It's the times when things
aren't going so well that you need to have
a sense of humor."

Will wasn't sure what humor meant, but
he would think about it. Maybe Larry Ett
had a good idea.

HOME
SWEET
HOME

14

But now it was time for Will to go to school. As he rode with his dad from the ranch he thought, "I wonder what school will be like. I wonder what I can rope there with my lariat."

"Oh, oh!" sighed Larry Ett. "Will's going to get into trouble again."

As it turned out, school wasn't a bit like the ranch. There weren't any calves to rope. "I'll just toss my rope over that statue," Will decided.

"Will! Be careful!" cried Larry Ett.

Will realized too late that the statue was not fastened to its base. "Oh, no!" he cried. The statue toppled over and smashed to pieces.

The other boys laughed. Will didn't think it was funny—especially since his father had to come and pay for the statue.

Determined to stay out of trouble, Will went off
alone to practice his roping. At least he thought he
was alone.

But look carefully. Can you see who is coming
around the corner of the school building? What do
you think is going to happen?

"Aaaagh!" Will's teacher choked. He got red in the face. He fell down. Then he got very, very angry!

"Oh, oh!" said Will. "I'm in trouble again!" Will helped his teacher up and took off the rope. Will apologized. "I didn't see you. It was a mistake."

"You've had your last chance!" roared the teacher. "You're expelled!"

"You'll laugh about this someday," whispered Larry Ett, "only I don't think you'd better do it now."

To Will, some of the things he did didn't seem that bad. But to grown-ups they seemed terrible. When his father found out what had happened he decided to send Will to a military academy where the rules were very strict.

When he arrived at Kemper Military School, Will had to smile, thinking back at what had happened. "I guess I did look pretty silly, lassoing my teacher. But I'm not going to do that again."

"Good boy," said Larry Ett. "When you can see the funny side of things, you feel better. And that lets you think better. You're really beginning to learn, Will."

Soon Will had a neat military uniform, like the other boys. They all liked to listen to him talk.

"You're very good at public speaking, Will," one teacher told him. "You have a good memory and a quick mind. You always make us laugh. And you give us something to think about. You win the medal for the best speaker in the school."

But deep down Will was still the boy who would rather play than work. He didn't study most subjects and so he did poorly in school. This made him very unhappy.

Then Will decided to do something very foolish. What do you think it was?

Will ran away from school. He climbed
out his window and lowered himself
down on his rope. "I'm quitting the
entire school business for life," Will said.

"I don't think this is a very good idea,
Will," warned Larry Ett. But Will wasn't
listening.

Because he didn't want to face his father,
he didn't go home. Roping was the thing
Will did best, so he went to a ranch and
got a job as a cowboy.

KEMPER

While he was a cowboy, Will got to practice his roping without getting into any trouble. His roping was getting better and better.

But being a cowboy and tending cattle was harder work than he thought. Both Larry Ett and Will were hot and dusty. It was so dusty you couldn't even see Larry Ett.

One day Larry Ett coughed and said, ''Why not go home, Will? Even if you did run away from school, your father will be glad to see you.''

Both Will and his dad were glad when Will came home. "Oooh!" sighed Will. "It feels so good to lie down in my own bed."

Larry Ett laughed. "Running away from school was sure one of your dumbest ideas, Will. You looked so silly."

Will smiled, but he didn't laugh.

Larry Ett chuckled. "Well, at least you're learning to smile at yourself when you make a mistake."

After a while, Will's dad said, "It's good to have you staying at home, Will. I hope working as a cowboy has taught you something. I have to be away on important business. While I'm gone you'll be the boss of the ranch. Make sure everyone does his job, Will."

What kind of a boss do you think Will was?

Will wasn't a very good boss. He built a stage on the ranch. He stood on the stage and practiced his rope tricks. He told funny stories and made the cowboys and cowgirls laugh. Will knew how to make people laugh. But he didn't know the first thing about making them work.

"Oh, no!" cried Will's father when he came back to the ranch. "Will, aren't you ever going to grow up and be responsible?"

26

"Sorry, Dad," said Will. "I guess I just don't want to be a ranch boss. I want to do what I'm good at."

So Will went off to join a rodeo.

You know what a rodeo is, don't you? Of course. It's a contest where cowhands can win money if they're the best at riding or roping.

At first Will was put into a cowboy band that helped entertain the rodeo customers.

"That's pretty funny," said Larry Ett. "You can't even play a musical instrument."

"It's very funny," Will laughed. Then he held a trombone to his lips and pretended to play it.

You see, the band was getting ready to play a joke on the other cowboys. As you can imagine, Will was looking forward to being a part of it.

The leader of the band called to the rough, tough cowboys who came to ride and rope in the rodeo. "I'll bet I have a cowboy in my band who can rope a calf faster than any of you real cowboys!"

"No way!" laughed the cowboys.

Will, who had been practicing his roping for a long time, thought, "Those cowboys are sure in for a surprise!"

The roping contest was held, and who do you think won?

29

Will won! The joke was on the cowboys.

"Hooray! Hooray!" everyone cheered. "Will Rogers is the best calf roper in the whole rodeo!"

"Nice going, Will!" shouted Larry Ett.

Will liked roping in the rodeo. But he also liked to go home every now and then.

On one of his trips home Will met someone special.

There was a new girl in town. Her name was Betty Blake.

"Wow!" thought Will. "She's the prettiest girl I've ever seen. I've got to make her notice me!"

Will tried to show off. He got his bicycle. He rode past Betty's house trying to stand on his head.

You know what happened, don't you? Yes. Will fell. He hurt himself. He was embarrassed, but he started to laugh.

"Say, it feels pretty good when I laugh at myself!" Will suddenly realized.

Larry Ett was so proud of Will. He and Betty laughed too. And what do you think Betty thought about a boy who could laugh at himself? "I like him a lot," she thought.

Will and Betty began to see a lot of each other. Will thought that one day he might marry Betty. But first he wanted to travel. Going on a boat to far-off places seemed like a good idea.

But when Will traveled by boat he got very seasick. "Oooh! I feel terrible!" Will groaned. Larry Ett didn't feel well either.

In time Will got over being seasick. He traveled to many faraway places. He went to England, South America, Africa, and Australia.

Will was a champion roper by now, and people paid money to watch him. He had fun traveling, and he learned something valuable. "Wherever they are, people are pretty much the same," Will realized.

When Will finally arrived back in the United States, he did something spectacular. What do you think it was?

Will was doing his roping act at a rodeo in New York. Suddenly a wild steer broke out of its pen. It crashed through the fence and charged into the audience. People screamed.

"That steer could kill someone!" Will thought.

He quickly whirled his rope through the air and around the steer's neck. Will dug his heels into the dirt. He pulled the rope tight.

How the crowd cheered then! "He saved us!" they shouted.

Will Rogers was a hero!

36

The next day Will's picture was in the New York newspapers.

"I'm famous," Will told Larry Ett. "I'll go get a job doing my rope tricks on the stage. Lots of people will pay money to see me now!"

But do you think it was going to be that easy for Will?

No! Most theater managers thought that rope tricks belonged in a rodeo, not on a New York stage.

"Sorry," they said to Will. "We can't use you."

It was a difficult time for Will. The rodeo had left town. Will had no job. "I was pretty silly to think I'd get work just because I had my picture in the paper," he said. Then he laughed at himself and he felt better.

At last Will persuaded one theater man to give him a chance. He could do his rope tricks. He could even take his pony on the stage.

The pony wore special rubber boots so it wouldn't slip and fall. But someone had left whipped cream on the floor of the stage. The pony slid across the stage and almost fell into the audience.

"That's pretty funny," said Will. "But I could hurt my pony this way." So from then on Will left the pony out of his act.

Then one night when Will was onstage something good happened to him. Will made a mistake! He tangled his rope around his legs.

Again Will looked silly, but now he could laugh at himself. He grinned and said, "A rope isn't so bad to get tangled up in—if it isn't around your neck."

The audience roared! They liked Will's sense of humor. They liked the way he made them laugh even more than they liked the way he roped.

Even though people liked him, Will felt lonely. There was someone special he wanted to be with.

So what do you think he decided to do?

Will went home to see Betty. He asked her to marry him. He was so happy when she said yes!

And who do you think Will pretended was the best man? It was Larry Ett, who winked and whispered, "This is fun being the best man. I'm glad Will and Betty decided to get married."

Later on Will told everybody, "The day I roped Betty I did the star performance of my life."

After they were married Will and Betty began to raise a family.

Of course, Will went on doing his roping act on the stage. But now he was talking more than he was roping. What he said was so funny that people came back again and again to hear what he would say next.

"I can't keep saying the same things," said Will to Betty. "I need new jokes all the time."

"Why don't you make jokes about the things you read in the newspaper everyday?" asked Betty.

"That's a great idea!" exclaimed Will. He tried out the idea right away.

"Well, all I know is what I read in the papers," Will would say onstage.

When Will talked, the audience laughed. They saw that there was a funny side to what happened to people in the newspapers. Then they began to see that there was probably a funny side to most of the things that happened to *them* too. They began to laugh at themselves. And they felt happier.

Will was also happy. At last he was doing the thing he really did best. He wasn't just twirling a rope. He was becoming a great humorist.

Do you know what a humorist is?

A humorist is someone who helps people see the funny side of what they're doing. And when they can do that, most people are not so afraid to make a mistake. They think more clearly. And they like themselves a lot better.

45

Will didn't usually get nervous when he did his act. But one night the theater manager almost had to push him onstage.

What made Will so nervous?

A friend said, "Will! Woodrow Wilson, the President of the United States, is in the audience!"

"Oh, no!" groaned Will. "I was going to tell some jokes about the President. Suppose he hasn't learned to laugh at himself? Suppose he gets angry?"

Will started his act. The audience listened. They didn't laugh out loud the way they usually did. They were watching the President to see what he would do.

First the President smiled. Then he chuckled. Then he laughed. He laughed so hard he almost fell out of his chair.

Then everyone else laughed. They really liked to see such an important person laughing at himself.

After the show was over President Wilson did something. What do you suppose he did?

The President of the United States went backstage to shake hands with Will Rogers. Even a President can enjoy seeing the funny side of what he is doing.

Larry Ett was a little shy when he saw the President come up to Will. He hid behind Will's legs. But after the President left, Will thought that he heard Larry Ett say, "Wouldn't your parents be proud of you tonight!"

Will knew that they would.

More and more people wanted to learn what Will had to say. They wanted to see the funny side of what was happening in the world and in their own lives.

So Will was asked to write a column for the newspapers. He was even asked to be in the movies!

It was hard work acting in the movies, but it was fun too. Will was happy.

Will was working hard and getting very good indeed at what he was doing—writing for the newspapers, appearing on stage, acting in the movies, and talking on the radio.

One day Will sat on the running board of his car typing his piece for the newspaper. Larry Ett looked over his shoulder. "You've worked very hard to develop your sense of humor, Will," he seemed to say. "No wonder you're so happy."

Many people heard Will speak on the radio. During a time called the Great Depression many people had no jobs and no money. They were very worried.

But when they gathered around the radios in their homes and listened to Will they had to laugh. Will's humor helped them get through some very difficult times.

Everybody felt better when they heard Will. Calvin Coolidge, who was once President of the United States, seldom smiled. But when he was with Will even he laughed and enjoyed himself.

Will Rogers met lots of famous people, including kings and queens and heads of state. They all enjoyed him and learned from his sense of humor.

But there were other people Will liked to be with just as much.

Will enjoyed meeting people who lived in small towns. He got the ideas for some of his best jokes when he listened carefully to what the people were saying.

But more than any other place, Will liked to be home on his ranch with his wife and children.

Will liked to sit outside with Betty and watch the children. They were learning to rope—something Will enjoyed doing all his life. Sometimes they made mistakes. Will would laugh.

"I hope our children learn to see the funny side of life," he would say to Betty. "They'll enjoy themselves more when they do."

Will remembered back to when he was a child. He thought, "It sure was fun to pretend that my rope was really Larry Ett. I learned so much, just listening to myself." Will could still imagine that Larry Ett was nearby.

But it was not always so peaceful and quiet for Will. All kinds of people liked to come to Will's ranch and visit him. He had lots of friends.

Do you know why so many people liked Will Rogers?

Because Will Rogers had a very good sense of humor. It even helped him to like people more. When they did silly things Will didn't mind. He just grinned.

In fact, he once said, "I never met a man I didn't like." And so, of course, everyone liked Will back.

Will's humor made him and everyone around him happier.

And what about you?

You may not be able to be famous, but you *can* do something just as important.

You can learn the value of humor.
Then you can be happier, too—
just like our humorous friend,
Will Rogers.

The End

William Penn Adair Rogers, the youngest of eight children, was born on November 4, 1879, in his parents' ranch house halfway between the towns of Claremore and Oologah in what was then Indian territory and is now the state of Oklahoma.

His father Clem was one-eighth Cherokee and his mother Mary, one-quarter Cherokee, which Will figured made him about "one-eighth cigar-store Injun."

Even the name of the state where he was born, Oklahoma, was derived from Indian words. (*Okla* means red and *homma* means people.) Will later said, "My ancestors didn't come over on the *Mayflower*. They met the boat."

Will's mother died when he was only ten years old. It was a great loss to Will, who missed her gentle manner, sense of humor, love of music, and easy way with people— some of the strongest traits inherited by her son.

The fun-loving son of a prosperous father, Will had every chance for a good education. But as bright as he was, Will wasn't interested in any of the many different schools he attended.

Will Rogers always spoke with a distinct Western drawl and a total disregard for proper English. When Will is quoted in this book, his words are paraphrased into language which most people feel is more appropriate for children to learn. His wife tried to encourage Will to speak properly, but Will always felt that his drawl was at least partially responsible for his unique success.

More than anything else though, it was Will's sense of humor that helped him succeed as philosopher, columnist, movie star, radio personality, philanthropist, and human being.

In 1899 Will met Betty Blake. They were married nine years later in Betty's hometown of Rogers, Arkansas. Betty was a great part of Will's life—his best critic, his financial and business manager, his partner, and his favorite person. Will and Betty had four children, but to their sorrow, one of their sons, Fred, died in infancy. Their three surviving children, Will, Jr., Jimmy, and Mary, were an important part of the Rogers' lives.

In 1905 Will met a fellow rodeo performer, Tom Mix, who talked of his travels to far-off

WILL ROGERS
1879–1935

China, and his days with Teddy Roosevelt's Rough Riders. These conversations kindled Will's desire to travel. And when Will wasn't at home with his family, he was usually traveling. He was a great promoter of two new modes of transportation: the automobile and the airplane. His friends included Henry Ford (who presented Will with the first Model A car) and most of the leading aviators of the time, including Billy Mitchell, Charles Lindbergh, and Wiley Post.

Will's life ended in 1935 on a flight around the world with Wiley Post. Their plane crashed in desolate Point Barrow, Alaska. The entire world mourned his death.

It was very risky to fly in those days. The airplane was just being developed. But Will had always been one to take risks. He once gave a friend the advice, "Go out on a limb. That's where the fruit is."

Will took chances when he poked fun at hypocrisy, smugness, and greed—even if they occurred in the most famous and important people. He did so with a good sense of humor, however. And people from every level of society loved him for it.

It is ironic that it was the humorist Will Rogers who said, "You must judge a man's greatness by how much he is missed."

THE VALUE OF BELIEVING IN YOURSELF	The Story of Louis Pasteur
THE VALUE OF DETERMINATION	The Story of Helen Keller
THE VALUE OF PATIENCE	The Story of the Wright Brothers
THE VALUE OF KINDNESS	The Story of Elizabeth Fry
THE VALUE OF TRUTH AND TRUST	The Story of Cochise
THE VALUE OF CARING	The Story of Eleanor Roosevelt
THE VALUE OF COURAGE	The Story of Jackie Robinson
THE VALUE OF CURIOSITY	The Story of Christopher Columbus
THE VALUE OF RESPECT	The Story of Abraham Lincoln
THE VALUE OF IMAGINATION	The Story of Charles Dickens
THE VALUE OF FAIRNESS	The Story of Nellie Bly
THE VALUE OF SAVING	The Story of Benjamin Franklin
THE VALUE OF LEARNING	The Story of Marie Curie
THE VALUE OF SHARING	The Story of the Mayo Brothers
THE VALUE OF RESPONSIBILITY	The Story of Ralph Bunche
THE VALUE OF HONESTY	The Story of Confucius
THE VALUE OF GIVING	The Story of Ludwig van Beethoven
THE VALUE OF UNDERSTANDING	The Story of Margaret Mead
THE VALUE OF LOVE	The Story of Johnny Appleseed
THE VALUE OF FANTASY	The Story of Hans Christian Andersen
THE VALUE OF FORESIGHT	The Story of Thomas Jefferson
THE VALUE OF HELPING	The Story of Harriet Tubman
THE VALUE OF DEDICATION	The Story of Albert Schweitzer
THE VALUE OF FRIENDSHIP	The Story of Jane Addams
THE VALUE OF ADVENTURE	The Story of Sacagawea